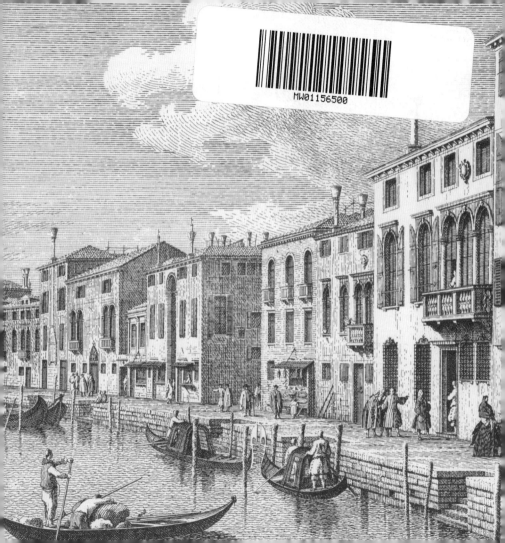

Also by Donna Leon

Venetian Curiosities

Donna Leon

Venetian Curiosities

with a Vivaldi CD by *Il Complesso Barocco*

WILLIAM HEINEMANN: LONDON

Published by William Heinemann 2012

2 4 6 8 10 9 7 5 3

First published in 2011 by Diogenes Verlag AG Zürich

First published in Great Britain in 2012 by
William Heinemann
Random House, 20 Vauxhall Bridge Road,
London SW1V 2SA

www.randomhouse.co.uk

Addresses for companies within The Random House Group Limited can be found at:
www.randomhouse.co.uk/offices.htm

The Random House Group Limited Reg. No. 954009

A CIP catalogue record for this book
is available from the British Library

ISBN 9780434022069

Printed and bound in the Uk by Butler Tanner & Dennis Ltd

Contents

Foreword

Just as the person coming to live in Venice has many physical realities to adjust to—walking, always walking; climbing up and down bridges and stairs; the delicate undulance of travel by water—they must also know about a kind of undulance in the accuracy with which events are reported: the further back in time the origin of the story, and the more retellings it has experienced, the rougher the waters of truth grow.

In Venice, the marketplace and the dinner table are two of the principal sites for the dissemination of (mis)information. Many of the stories told by Venetians about their city pass through either or both of these sites, and in them, over the decades, I've heard many variants of a story that deals with how some people still living here behaved during the war. Enough time has passed for every Venetian to have been re-

9

minted as an ardent member of the Resistance, so overt collaboration is seldom a subject; instead, this story remains true to that age-old Venetian theme: sharp business dealings. On six occasions, and from six different people of three separate nationalities, I have heard a story that recounts the purchase for almost nothing of a portfolio of Tiepolo drawings (with the variant of "selected Old Master prints") from someone who is reported to have been both a man and a woman and both a Jew and a Christian, but who was always desperate to sell the drawings. The constants are the name of the purchaser, the fact that he took advantage of the misery and desperation of the seller, the current location of the drawings, and the underlying duplicity of the deal.

Think of a risotto. It begins with *un fondo,* the basis of the dish, which can be made of anything: asparagus, shrimp, pumpkin, even simple broth. As the risotto cooks, other things get stirred in, each new ingredient changing the taste. Finally, toss in some rice and add boiling broth. More broth, and let it boil until it's done. Or start with rumor; if you prefer, start with fact, keep adding and keep stirring: the taste is sure to change with each new ingredient. In the end, you will have risotto, or you will have Venetian curiosities.

Because Venetians were, and remain, merchants, they are also fierce and devoted keepers of records: some of the documents in the Archivio di Stato date back a thousand years. The aisles in the Archivio are reported to fill some three hundred rooms and the shelves are said to run for seventy kilometers. Contained therein—along with official governmental decrees and private historical accounts as well as the reports of spies and the police—are the records from civil and judicial authorities that report, with rigorous accuracy, those events that led to legal actions, the decisions of the judges, and the consequences of those decisions.

The stories recounted in *Venetian Curiosities* have their origin in the Archivio and in the records that Venetians have been depositing there for a millennium. The versions we hear or read today, however, have been added to and neatened up by centuries of rumor and retelling. Today's reader would perhaps find strange the casual reference to torture as a sure way of finding the truth and the equally casual assumption that persons of high estate were—as Orwell would have it—"more equal" than other citizens, were it not for the return to fashion of the first belief and the continued endurance of the second. These strange stories of the city, or perhaps more accurately, these stories of a strange city, will, it is hoped, suggest the ways in which the constancy of human nature makes us resemble these people who, centuries ago, acted and suffered their way through life in this wondrous city.

Many of the curious things that happened in Venice and the odd creatures who passed through the city were painted by Pietro Longhi, an eighteenth-century artist who delighted in showing his fellow Venetians what they and their city looked like. Longhi was a master storyteller. He picks out scenes from daily life and shows us their often candlelit normalcy, leaving us to create the story that might make them make sense. In his paintings can be found the famous rhinoceros, countless ordinary dogs, mice, and monkeys. He left us a portrait of Magrat, the famous Nordic giant, captured in his red-suited glory, as well as of less conspicuous residents of the city, most of them engaged in the unexciting business of their daily lives.

Canaletto is certainly the most famous painter of Venice (as different from the most famous Venetian painter). Unlike

Longhi, who remains indoors, Canaletto takes us outside and flaunts stunning long views of the exterior beauty of the sun-swept city. At times almost photorealistic, Canaletto's grand paintings show the city in its most attractive light, a vision likely to appeal to his wealthy Northern European clients, who wanted this record of light and life to take back home to their darker countries. He also produced *capricci,* curious paintings of buildings that did not exist in Venice or that he had arbitrarily moved from their real location to some other part of the city.

The story of the life of Vivaldi, Venice's most famous composer, like so many Venetian curiosities, is told in official documents and stories that are known, or believed, to be true. The record of his birth is kept in the church of San Giovanni in Bragora: the register is there to be seen. There is the date of his ordination as a priest, 1703, as well as the dates of the composition and first performance of some of his works. And then there are the stories that have become legends: he ran from the altar while saying mass and never said mass again; he was or was not the lover of Anna Giro, one of the singers who worked most frequently with him and who lived with him during the last years of his life; he died and was buried in a pauper's grave in Vienna. The blending of fact and invention, of truth and something more appealing, serves as a perfect example of the undulant nature of truth in Venice and make Vivaldi, beyond his musical genius, a true son of La Serenissima.

Like Longhi, Vivaldi captured the rhythm and energy of the city, those qualities that exerted such a strong pull on the people who flocked to Venice as visitors. And like Longhi, Vivaldi put into his art what was close to hand: the instruments played by the students in the orchestra he led, and often along with those instruments, their young voices.

One thing is sure: Vivaldi wrote concerti for instruments and combinations of instruments that surprise and delight his listeners. A decorative society is always in search of something new; La Serenissima was endlessly hungry for *divertimenti* of any sort. Vivaldi was more than ready, and gloriously able, to serve his fellow Venetians a seemingly endless feast of new and amazing music. These concerti are but a small part of the banquet he prepared for his listeners.

History and events have demoted Venice from its position as one of the most powerful cities of Europe, but the genius of artists like Longhi, Vivaldi, and Canaletto, with their lasting proof of the city's lust for pleasure and beauty, will keep its memory alive forever.

The Elephant Goes to Church

Years ago, I was told that there is an ordinance in Venice that prohibits the keeping of chickens inside the city limits, a nugget of interesting information about the past. The rooster of San Marco? I think not. One has but to read the memoirs of people who visited or lived here in former centuries to be aware of the animals, both real and imaginary, that shared the city with them. Many accounts tell of people moving about on horseback, and one need only glance at some of the stone panels set into the walls of buildings to see images of bees, griffins, fish, and an endless parade of lions. And then, as now, there were the rats, which Venetians attempt to render less horrid by calling "*pantegane*."

Venice's painters, as well, left a record of animals: Carpaccio's bored prostitutes try desultorily to entertain their equally bored dogs; Saint Jerome is always accompanied by his faithful dog; two evangelists are pictured as animals; the area at the feet of Negroponte's Virgin in the church of San Francesco della Vigna, is filled with tranquil birds.

The archives report on other animals whose presence in the city is as strange as that of the griffin. During the Carnevale season that stretched from 1818 to 1819 (note how long Carnevale spread itself out two hundred years ago) an elephant was brought to the city, the better to delight the royal guests: Francis I, Emperor of Austria, and his fourth wife, Carolina, along with some of their children.

Part of the entertainment prepared for them by their not very loyal Venetian citizens was a naval review, during which repeated artillery salvos fired in honor of the royal presence were so strong as to require the navy to repay local residents for damage done to their house facades and chimneys. Unfortunately, a male elephant, part of the group brought to the city for Carnevale, was being kept somewhere along the Riva degli Schiavoni, and the sound of the artillery provoked him to "outrageous ferocity."

The elephant's increasingly violent behavior, worsened by the approach of springtime that awoke his "amorous instinct," led to the decision that it was time to remove the elephant from the city before his violence became uncontrollable. For this purpose, an enormous boat was brought to the *riva* on the morning of March 15, 1819, and the elephant was encouraged to walk on board. But the water was rough and the gangplank unsteady, and so the elephant, though he tried four times to go on board, finally retreated to the embankment and refused to continue, whereupon he was taken to a storeroom on the *riva* and confined therein.

In the middle of the night, the elephant again grew violent and Camillo Rosa, his custodian, was summoned to calm him. But the elephant, by now driven past all patience, picked Rosa up with his trunk and hurled him against the wall and then, to make sure, stepped on him.

Then the elephant broke loose and ran toward the bridge of Ca' di Dio. Not liking the idea of having to cross a bridge, he turned around and, after breaking into a fruit stall to eat and drink a caffè (it's in the records) he made toward Calle del Dose, across Campo della Bragora, and up Salizada Sant'Antonin. He ran into a dead-end *calle,* emerged, and ran toward the bridge of Sant'Antonin but, again demonstrating his aversion to bridges, refused to climb it and somehow managed to break into a nearby church. During all of this, soldiers had been firing their rifles at him, but the thickness of his skin prevented their bullets from doing any harm.

There followed a consultation during which the various civil, military, and ecclesiastical authorities decided what was to be done, and finally a cannon was sent from the Arsenale. During all of this, the elephant made good use of his time in the church, moving benches around to build himself a kind of nest or fortress in front of the main altar. But then the elephant's weight shattered one of the tombstones in the floor of the church, trapping his foot.

After the arrival of the cannon, a hole was bored in the side wall of the church. There were two shots, and then—at four minutes after eight in the morning—the elephant fell dead in *un lago di sangue*. At five in the afternoon, the body of the elephant was taken out to the Lido, where it was to be buried, the same way that old fruit and vegetables were.

But by seven o'clock that evening the burial order had been countermanded and the body was sent to the deconsecrated church of San Biasio. There, after a day of bargaining

and discussion, the elephant was sold, for 800 florins (2,080 Italian lira) to the Natural History Museum of the University of Padova. And so, in the church, the elephant was skinned and eviscerated, this work possible only so long as the church was filled with sufficient quantities of oxygenated hydrochloric acid, vinegar, burning pitch, and aquavit to overcome the smells.

A hundred years later, the skin of the elephant, now reduced to a moth-eaten ruin, was hurled from a window of the Padova museum into the courtyard below, where it was picked up by the children of the neighborhood, who played with it until they sold it to a local man, who in his turn exhibited it until its "final destruction."

A Palazzo on the Turn of a Card

"The art of losing isn't hard to master." It is unlikely that the American poet Elizabeth Bishop had Renaissance Venice's invention of organized and legalized gambling in mind when she wrote that line, but it does speak a simple truth about the Venetians' historical fascination with gambling, which seems to be part of their DNA. Many Venetians grow misty-eyed when they tell the story of some ancestor who lost the family palazzo or business on the turn of a card or speak of friends whose families were destroyed by an ancestor who could not resist the urge to gamble.

Until the sixteenth century, gambling was pretty much a private concern, conducted in backstreets and considered not at all respectable. In a first attempt to control the vice, city authorities forbade gambling in any secret place or anywhere a woman of easy virtue might be present. Prohibitive laws, however, were helpless to stem its growing popularity and thus the rulers of the city grew nervous about the effect upon the families of those—especially the aristocratic and wealthy—who gambled away their patrimony, thus condemning their wives and children to starvation and misery. Punishments of increasing severity were imposed—including imprisonment, exile, and the loss of nose and ears—all to no avail, as is often the case when only part of a population perceives an activity to be a vice. Indeed, in 1626, a subdeacon actually went so far as to baptize a playing card in the hopes that its Christianization would bring its owner luck.

Venetians are pragmatic people and have a deep sympathy with human weakness, matched with a keen understanding of the marketplace, and so in 1638, La Serenissima decided to bow in the face of the inevitable and open the Ridotto, in Palazzo Dandolo, near Campo San Moise, where food and drink would be offered to men who could gamble openly and where city authorities could keep an eye on the action. More importantly, they got a cut of the take, since the rules of the games were heavily in favour of the house or dealer, and the house and dealer were now in the hands of the city administration.

One can theorize that since military prowess was no longer a characteristic of the Venetian aristocracy, their manhood sought a means of proving itself through gambling. Why else the almost obsessive disregard with which so many of them conspired in the destruction of their family's past and future? From one moment to the next, palazzi that had for centuries been in the control of one family passed to some other family, and futures that had been secure were consigned to ruin. More interestingly, many contemporary accounts seem to admire this behavior.

Casanova writes often of his fascination with and inability to resist the lure of gambling, stating that he was "relaxed and smiling when I lost, and I won without covetousness." A common intoxication with risk, loss, and losing is evident in other cultures. Is not "The Charge of the Light Brigade"—a commemoration of one of the worst debacles in British military history—also one of the most famous poems in the language? How else explain the fascination with Russian roulette? The unifying element is the necessity not to be seen to care: the art of losing must not seem hard to master.

Another explanation might lie in the origins of the power of Venice, which is securely lodged in trade as much as in military might; indeed, its most famous families began as merchants, not warriors, and many of its most famous warriors were mercenaries and not Venetians. If personal and family status is created by the acquisition of wealth through trade, then cavalier disregard of the loss of that wealth at the whim of fortune will be seen as equal to courage on the battlefield in the face of the enemy. Perhaps to the merchant mind the loss of a fortune equals the loss of a life.

A desire to take risks seems to have been part of Vivaldi's nature: how better to assure a topsy-turvy life than by becoming an opera impresario? During his career, he traveled widely to perform his music and produce his operas, following the market for decades—to Florence, Prague, Rome, and Amsterdam—while at the same time turning out music for the court of France.

Like any gambler, Vivaldi won and spent fortunes, and as happens with many gamblers, his luck finally ran out. Late in his life, he left Venice in hopes of finding success and fortune in Vienna. But he found no wealthy patron, only, as did Mozart a century later, an anonymous pauper's grave.

Prostitutes Working for the Good of the State

Venice, even now, is known for the excess of its beauty: where else is so much of it packed into such a small space? In what other city is the beauty of almost everything in sight so overwhelming and excessive?

During much of its history, the artistic glory of La Serenissima was not the only sort of excess a person could find. Carnevale seemed to be in a permanent state of temporal expansion and came to fill much of the year, allowing residents and visitors to move around the city cloaked and masked and thus to enjoy the opportunities provided by anonymity.

One consequence of this anonymity was the ability to seek the company of the prostitutes of Venice, the fame of whose beauty and charms—like that of their city—expanded throughout Europe and served as a great tourist attraction. Not for the last time, city authorities displayed a double-faced attitude toward tourism; not for the last time they demonstrated a certain disdain for the motives that brought these tourists to the city while at the same time doing everything to encourage more of them to come, quite happily pocketing the money they brought with them.

Tolerance went hand in hand with an attempt to contain the prostitutes or *meretrici,* at least geographically: the city tried to limit them to Castelletto, an area not far from the Rialto, where houses were rented to them by noble families and where the same families are today renting the same houses to wealthy tourists. This policy proved—not surprisingly—ineffective and thus, in 1412, the authorities passed more stringent laws, forcing the growing number of prostitutes to live in the area around a house left to the city by the Rampani family. In this area, called Carampane, the prostitutes were controlled by strict laws governing their movements and behavior. They had to observe a curfew, could not work on certain holy days, and could walk around freely only on Saturday and then only when wearing a yellow scarf. Prostitutes who violated these rules were flogged; the archives are silent on the consequences to their clients.

However much the city might condemn the prostitutes publicly, the authorities were not above invoking their aid in moments of perceived peril to the city, and so during the Renaissance, they appealed to the women's patriotism to help overcome the menace presented by male homosexuality, said to be rampant. To encourage young Venetian men in the right sort of heir-producing sexuality, prostitutes were enjoined to expose their breasts on windowsills and bridges—thus "Ponte delle Tette"—and windows and were even allowed to illuminate the curious spectacle with lanterns. One has but to observe the mammary excesses of Italian magazines today to realize that certain advertising techniques never change: regardless of the product, the sight of tits and ass still encourages people to buy.

Along with selling, merchants also like to count things up and write down the number. Earnings, losses, beads, fish, boots. The city of merchants had a love affair with numbers and so, in 1509, they counted 11,164 prostitutes living within the city. A little more than a hundred years later—sodomy apparently having been extirpated—they abandoned counting in favor of promulgating more rules for the prostitutes to obey. The new rules forbade them from living on the Grand Canal or traveling in a boat with more than two oars. They could not wear jewelry, pearls, or gold, or enter a church during Mass. More importantly, at least from a legal point of view, they could not press a case against a man who did not pay them for services, nor could they give witness in a court of law.

Regardless of these restrictions, some women did manage to climb up the ladder of success and earn the name of *cortegiana,* or courtesan. Among these was the famous Veronica Franco, born in Venice around the year 1546. Though married young to a doctor, she soon turned to prostitution. She was, however, a woman of great talent, charm, and beauty; among her many admirers was King Henri III of France who, after a visit to her, wanted to take from Venice at least a portrait of her.

Her friends included artists, musicians, and writers, and she herself was considered a more than adequate poet. At the age of forty, however, she decided to change her way of life and founded, near the Carmine, a House of Help, where refuge was offered to prostitutes who, like their patroness, wanted to change their lives. Some married, some took religious vows, and some retired to live with families. Soon before her death, in 1580, Franco wrote to a mother who wanted her daughter to become a prostitute. Of her former profession, she had this to say: "It is so unhappy and against the sense of humanity to oblige the body to such servitude that the mere thought is terrifying."

The Truth Is What You Choose It to Be

Any foreigner who lives in Italy long enough (ten minutes will suffice) will come upon the word *dietrologia*. Roughly translated, this refers to the science of discovering what stands behind things or, in simpler terms, the science of finding out what really caused things to happen. Just as Italians cannot abandon their belief that the common cold is transmitted only by *un corrente d'aria,* they are similarly incapable of believing any official explanation of events, preferring to seek more arcane or sinister causes. Even the most cursory reading of their history, ancient or recent, suggests that this might indeed be the path to wisdom.

An example of cloudy motivation is to be found in the story of Antonio Foscarini, son of one of Venice's most illustrious families. His career began splendidly: he was Venetian ambassador to both the courts of King Henry IV of

France and James I of England. In 1615, however, Foscarini was called back to Venice, accused of treason with Spain by his secretary, and imprisoned for three years while the charge was examined. In 1618, he was fully exonerated, released from prison, and restored to his seat in the Senate with full honors. The secretary was sentenced to only two years in prison for calumny.

In 1622, Foscarini was again accused of treason with Venice's then-enemy Spain, this time by two agents of the Inquisition. He was arrested, imprisoned, condemned, strangled (he was a nobleman so there could be no public execution in front of the lower classes), and hung from one foot between the columns of San Marco and San Teodoro.

Less than a year later, the Council of Ten, which ruled La Serenissima, published a full exoneration of Foscarini, admitting that the unanimous condemnation had been mistaken. His denouncers were tried and convicted of false accusation, but before they could give any explanation of their crime, or tell who might have been behind it, they were hanged. Since then, historians have contrasted the conservative politics of the council that condemned Foscarini with the more liberal politics of the one that voted to exonerate him and have explained the two actions as responses to various religious and political forces then current in Europe.

Common belief, however, as is often the case, has found a more simple explanation, at least for Foscarini's failure to defend himself: love, or at least lust. The palazzo that he had been seen entering, supposedly to pass state secrets to his Spanish handlers, was also the home of the Countess of Arundel, wife of Thomas Howard, 2nd Earl of Arundel, a man whose high position at the English court would have made their meeting with Foscarini during his time in London inevitable.

In the accusation that led to his death, Foscarini was said to have entered the house of foreign enemies "in disguise and in normal dress," and to have been in their company "by day and by night." In a city famous for the disguises common to Carnevale, would not a lover sometimes wear it to visit his mistress?

The Countess of Arundel denied the story absolutely.

The facts remain: Foscarini was falsely accused, he either was given a chance to defend himself or he chose not to (the records are missing), he died, and his supposed lover—

married to an earl and mother of two children—denied the affair.

Comparison can be made to the cloud of unknowing that covers the nature of Vivaldi's relationship with Anna Giro, a singer whose life, both professional and personal, was linked to his. In 1720, upon Vivaldi's return to Venice from Mantua, Anna Giro came to live with him as his housekeeper. That fact can be interpreted in one way until it is revealed that her sister Paolina came along with her and lived with them.

In 1730, Giro traveled to Prague with Vivaldi. But so did his father. Though Vivaldi was occasionally criticized for living with a woman, he was never deprived of his priestly state because of it. The pieces of information can be interpreted to mean one thing, but then they can be interpreted to mean something else. Like the haunting strains of Vivaldi's music, the rhythms of *dietrologia,* once heard, are impossible to ignore or forget.

The Price of Lavish Beauty

One constant that runs through what the visitors and tourists to Venice have been writing for centuries is their description of the luxury and profligacy of life in the city. There is the story of the family that tossed golden plates out the window and into the waters of the canal after every gala meal, the better to impress their guests with their contempt for their own bottomless wealth. (The same stories, of course, sometimes fail to mention the fish nets spread across the canals beneath the windows to catch the plates and platters.) The wealth of Asia passed through the storehouses of Venice on its way to the rest of Europe, and young men attended parties dressed in cloth of gold and silk.

Because Venice had captured the trading routes to the Orient, the city grew fabulously wealthy, and by the sixteenth century, its wealth and decadence had made it a synonym for luxury and excess. Would it be possible today—even with the architectural and engineering skills available—to build this city as it is? Outside of Las Vegas, that is.

But Venetians are, and remain, merchants, and merchants, no matter how much they might favor consumption, are always made nervous by waste. Reading contemporary accounts, one is often struck by a sense that, no matter how much they vaunted their extravagance, Venetians were always left uncomfortable by the nagging thought that all the money spent on splendor might better have been sunk back into the business. Sweet cakes wrapped in gold foil are no doubt an impressive proof of a family's wealth, but wouldn't it have been wiser to invest all that money in new barrels?

Along with their love of luxury, Venetians seem to have had an equally strong love for law and lawmaking. Thus they devised legal ways of controlling even the tiniest crevices of private life: who could live where, and with whom; who could vote or hold office; who could or could not enter a church. Every so often, as if suffering from a collective malarial fever caused by the visible evidence of their own wealth, the rulers passed sumptuary laws in an attempt to control their own reckless spending.

The choice of clothing is one of the easiest and most obvious ways to display wealth: why else pay 3,000 euros for a leather handbag? Aware of this constant in human behavior, the rulers of La Serenissima tried early on to limit the pomp with which a person could bedeck himself or his family. In 1511, a law was passed that limited the amount that could be spent on ornaments to the head or neck to fifty ducats on a single strand of pearls, worn at a neckline that could not be "ornamented in any other way." The quantity of cloth used in sleeves was also limited, and they were not allowed to be "slashed or open at any point, nor ornamented in any other way." No detail escaped: "The total value of all rings for the fingers may not exceed 400 ducats."

Not content with dictating what a person could wear outside the house, the makers of the law moved their concerns inside the homes and palazzi of their citizens, declaring that "one may not put on beds or use sheets embroidered with gold, silver, or silk, nor pillow slips, nor pillows, nor blankets, nor bedspreads, nor any other type of bedclothes adorned with gold, silver, jewels, nor may they be made of velvet, satin, or heavy silk." (Other than by suborning the maids or seducing the owner's wife, how did the makers of these laws plan to check that these laws were being obeyed? And who but a masochistic anchorite with a sense of style would choose to sleep on jewel-embroidered velvet sheets?)

An occasion where wealth *was* allowed to be conspicuously displayed was a wedding, when both families sought to give palpable evidence of their respective fortunes. A law passed in 1526, however, limited the value of wedding gifts that might be given to the groom, just as it restricted the number of suppers that might be offered him prior to the wedding. Further, it forbade the serving at these dinners of "partridge, pheasant, peacocks, and baby doves." Nor could large nut cakes be served, nor marzipan fruitcakes and sugared fruit. Fines were stipulated for both the guests and for the pastry chefs, just as fines were imposed for excessive ornamentation in dress.

Which brings us to a possible explanation of this particular Venetian curiosity. The fines imposed—some of them quite heavy—were to be paid to the State. These heavy fines, however, did little to stop the Venetians from bedecking

themselves and their houses just as they pleased. Move to the other side of Europe for a moment and consider the English duke whose castle was surrounded by endless acres planted with nothing but inedible—at least by humans—grass. The vast parks of the English aristocracy: what are they if not yet another example of conspicuous consumption?

The nobles of Venice had their origins in the merchant class, where everything exists to turn a profit. Why then not impose fines as a sort of luxury tax? This way, the visible evidence of wealth served a double purpose: it awed with its display of the wealth needed to buy the forbidden objects while, at the same time, the ability to pay the fines gave further evidence of that wealth. This is the realization of a merchant's dreams: pay for one and get one free.

Your Honor the Judge: Remember the Poor Young Baker

Just because you find it on the street doesn't mean it's yours
or that it's good luck to find it; this was as true in the sixteenth century as it is today. In the earliest hours of a cold
March morning in 1507, Piero, the son and apprentice of the
baker (and thus the name history has given him—Il Povaro
Fornaretto) in Calle de la Mandola, was on his way to work
(by way of the Bridge of the Assassins, please note) when his
eye fell upon something bright and glittering on the street.
He picked it up and discovered that it was the silver sheathe
of a knife.

Innocent Piero, overjoyed by his discovery, ran to show it
to his *ragazza,* Annella, who worked nearby. Holding it out
for her to examine, Piero declared that it would bring them
fortune and pay for their wedding. But she, less optimistic,
told him to take it back immediately to the place where he

had found it in case its rightful owner was looking for it.

Though confused by her words and fears, Piero hastened to do as she said and returned to the place where he had found the sheathe. At the angle beside the bridge, Piero saw the limp figure of a man lying on the ground and, believing he must be drunk, bent to try to help him. When he turned him over, however, Piero saw that the man was dead; worse, he saw that blood had spilled from his side; worst, the blood stained Piero's white baker's apron. Looking closer, he recognized the victim as Alvise Guorno, cousin and frequent visitor of Clemenza Barbo, the wife of Annella's employer.

Dawn was approaching by then, and two people—a woman at a window, and a local carpenter—saw Piero at the same moment: sheathe in hand, bloody apron, dead man lying at his feet. And they responded as would any respectable person of the lower classes: they told him to run and hide. But it was too late: the city patrol passed by and arrested Piero, who was quickly tortured into confessing and was thus condemned to be decapitated and his body cut in quarters.

Just as Piero was to be executed between the columns of San Teodoro and San Marco, a servant dashed from the house of Annella's employer with the news that the jealous husband had confessed the murder to his wife. The servant ran through the city, crying out the news of Piero's innocence but as he arrived in Piazza San Marco, a louder voice cried out, "*Giudizia e fatta!*" Piero was no more.

The story of the injustice of Piero's death does not appear in any of the official records of the city; it survives only in the legends that come down in the voices and memories of the people and in a common admonition often given by lawyers to judges, enjoining them to consider the consequences of mistaken verdicts and remember the poor baker.

Another part of the legend explains that, in the basilica, there is an oil-burning lamp that is never allowed to be extinguished: it is the lamp that is meant to remind the city of the innocence of Il Povaro Fornareto. Though I have asked custodians where it is and have looked for such a thing numerous times, I have yet to locate it.

Il Casotto del Lione,
Veduto in Venezia
Nel Carneuale del M.T. 67..
Dipinео dal Naturale
Da Pietro Longhi.

Diabolical Lust

Italy is a country exploding with every sort of richness. Aside from the gentle climate and fertile earth, history bursts with its achievements: the Renaissance, the opera, the Roman Empire, the Baroque. It has blessed the world with names to be remembered and commemorated: Verdi, Michelangelo, Rossini, Dante, Garibaldi. Indeed, these names are immortalized all over the country in *piazze, strade, vie,* and *campi* that pay geographical homage to these figures. It is virtually impossible to find a major Italian city without its Via Donizetti, Piazza Petrarca, Viale Leonardo da Vinci.

In Venice, however, things are a bit different, an example of which is seen at the first vaporetto stop the beauty-struck tourist reaches after leaving the train station and heading in the direction of the unworldly loveliness that awaits him.

Riva di Biasio. Biasio? Hmmm, and just who is this Biasio? Could it be Saint Biagio (aka Blaise), an Armenian bishop who is believed to have been beaten to death with carding combs in 316? He is the protector of throats and is to be invoked for help in removing objects lodged there. However useful this information—or his help—might be, his church is down in Castello, and so this is not the Biasio after whom the vaporetto stop is named.

That honor, it is reported in the Registri dei Giustiziati (record of the punished), is reserved for Biasio Cargnio (or Cargnico) a sixteenth-century *luganegher* (sausage maker) with a shop above this *riva*. Famous throughout the city, Biasio's *squazzetto*, a kind of rich meat stew, drew diners from all over the city. Until, that is, one day a hungry worker discovered the last digit of a finger—complete with a tiny fingernail—in his bowl. And it was only then that people remembered how small children had, of late, been disappearing from this part of the city. The writer of one account was careful enough to point out that this *squazzetto* was a dish much favored by the plebians, no doubt to remove any suspicion that the upper classes might sink, however accidentally, to eating such a thing. There is an uncomfortable lack of information about how long Cargnio had been using this recipe before the discovery of the fingernail. (Everything is in the details.)

The authorities were informed and the *luganegher* was arrested and quickly confessed to his "diabolical lust," after which he was taken back to his shop. His hands were cut off and he was dragged to Piazza San Marco at the tail of a horse, where he was decapitated between the columns in front of the basilica. He was then cut into four pieces and his body exposed. His house and shop were razed to the ground but his name could not so easily be eliminated, hence the Riva di Biasio.

Or perhaps not. Tassini, one of the most famous compilers of the stories and legends of Venice, notes that already in 1395, more than a century before Biasio opened for business, a reference was made in Latin to an event which took place at "ripam Biasii." The tides flow in and out of the *laguna,* floating things in and floating them away. Undulant, undulant truth.

Illustration Credits

40/41 Giovanni Antonio Canal, *The Grand Canal near the Rialto Bridge,* c. 1730.
Photo: copyright © Museum of Fine Arts, Houston, Texas, USA / Robert Lee Blaffer Memorial Collection, gift of Sarah Campbell Blaffer / Bridgeman Berlin

42 Pietro Longhi, *The Meeting,* probably 1746 (detail).
Photo: copyright © The Metropolitan Museum of Art / Bildagentur Preussischer Kulturbesitz

47 After Pietro Longhi, *The Declaration,* 1750 (detail).
Photo: copyright © Archivio Alinari, Florence

48/49 Giovanni Antonio Canal, *A Regatta on the Grand Canal,* 1732 (detail).
Photo: copyright © Peter Willi / Arthotek

50 Pietro Longhi, *La Toeletta,* c. 1750.
Photo: copyright © Erich Lessing / akg-images

55+57 Two details from Pietro Longhi, *The Banquet at Casa Nani, Given in Honor of their Guest, Clemente Augusto, Elector Archbishop of Cologne, on September 9, 1755,* (detail).
Photo: copyright © Ca' Rezzonico, Museo del Settecento, Venice / Alinari / Bridgeman Berlin

58/59   Giovanni Antonio Canal, *View of the Canal of Santa Chiara, Venice*.
        Photo: copyright © Musée Cognacq-Jay, Paris, France /
        Giraudon / Bridgeman Berlin

60   Anonymous painter, *Tavola della corporazione dei fornai,* 1730
        (detail).
        Photo: copyright © Cameraphoto/akg-images

64/65   After Pietro Longhi, *The Kitchen* (detail).
        Photo: copyright © Casa Goldoni, Venedig / 2011 Scala, Florence

66   Pietro Longhi, *Il casotto del Leone,* 1762.
        Photo: copyright © Cameraphoto/akg-images

82   Cristoforo Munari, *Still Life with Musical Instruments* (detail).
        Photo: copyright © Sopritendenza Florenz / 2011 Scala,
        Florence. Courtesy of Ministero per i Beni e le Attività Culturali

End papers: "Prospectus in Magnum Canalem e Regione S. Clarae ad
Aedem S. Crucis" in: Urbis Venetiarum prospectus celebriores ex Anto-
nii Canal tabulis XXXVIII. Aere expressi ab Antonio Visentini in partes
tres distributi. Pars prima, Venetiis, Apud Joannem Baptistam Pasqualis,
1742-1751. Courtesy of Ministero per i Beni e le Attività Culturali -
Biblioteca Nazionale Marciana. All rights reserved.

Music Credits

All music composed by Antonio Vivaldi (1678-1741).

Concerto for violin in E minor, "Il favorito," RV 277
[1] *Allegro*	4.40
[2] *Andante*	3.47
[3] *Allegro*	4.14

Riccardo Minasi, violin

Concerto for cello in C major, RV 398
[4] *Allegro*	3.06
[5] *Largo*	2.01
[6] *Allegro*	2.34

Marco Ceccato, cello

Concerto for oboe and bassoon in G major, RV 545
[7] *Andante molto*   3.29
[8] *Largo*   2.34
[9] *Allegro molto*   3.03

Patrick Beaugiraud, oboe
Carles Cristóbal, bassoon

Concerto for bassoon in F major, RV 489
[10] *Allegro*   3.49
[11] *Largo*   3.31
[12] *Allegro*   3.34

Carles Cristóbal, bassoon

Concerto for strings in D minor, "Madrigalesco," RV 129
[13] *Adagio*   1.08
[14] *Allegro*   2.14
[15] *Adagio*   0.56
[16] *Allegro*   1.18

Riccardo Minasi and Guadalupe del Moral, violins
Giulio D'Alessio, viola
Marco Ceccato, cello
Riccardo Coelati Rama, double bass
Andrea Perugi, harpsichord

Concerto for oboe in C major, RV 448
[17] *Allegro non molto*   4.19
[18] *Larghetto*   3.29
[19] *Allegro*   2.57

Patrick Beaugiraud, oboe

Concerto for violin in B minor, RV 386
[20] *Allegro*   4.37
[21] *Adagio*   3.10
[22] *Allegro*   2.51

Dmitry Sinkovsky, violin

Il Complesso Barocco: Cast

Riccardo Minasi, violin and concertmaster

Dmitry Sinkovsky, violin
Patrick Beaugiraud, oboe
Carles Cristóbal, bassoon
Marco Ceccato, cello

Riccardo Minasi, first violin
Alfia Bakieva, first violin
Guadalupe del Moral, first violin
Laura Mirri, first violin

Ana Liz Ojeda, second violin
Boris Begelman, second violin
Barbara Altobello, second violin

Giulio D'Alessio, viola
Isabella Bison, viola

Marco Ceccato, cello
Ludovico Takeshi Minasi, cello

Riccardo Coelati Rama, double bass
Andrea Perugi, harpsichord

Donna Leon was born in New Jersey in 1942 but she has lived in Venice since 1981. Commissario Guido Brunetti has brought Leon international fame, but baroque music is no less important to her. In 2011, she was named the honorary president of the Venetian Centre for Baroque Music, which is devoted to the promotion and dissemination of baroque music in all of its many forms.

Il Complesso Barocco founded in 1979 by Alan Curtis, is an international ensemble dedicated to baroque music on original instruments. The musicians have played an important role in the rediscovery of baroque opera from Monteverdi, to Handel, to Vivaldi, and have made a name for themselves through their original recordings. In 1997, the ensemble was awarded the Antonio Vivaldi International Recording Prize. In 2003, Il Complesso Barocco was awarded the German Record Critics' Award. The ensemble has also been awarded the International Handel Recording Prize on several occasions.